THE CHRISTIAN D

The Lutheran Church

by Roy Long

FOREWORD BY
THE ARCHBISHOP OF CANTERBURY

RELIGIOUS AND MORAL EDUCATION PRESS
An Imprint of Arnold-Wheaton

Religious and Moral Education Press
An Imprint of Arnold-Wheaton
Hennock Road, Exeter EX2 8RP

Pergamon Press Ltd
Headington Hill Hall, Oxford OX3 0BW

Pergamon Press Inc.
Maxwell House, Fairview Park, Elmsford,
New York 10523

Pergamon Press Canada Ltd
Suite 104, 150 Consumers Road, Willowdale,
Ontario M2J 1P9

Pergamon Press (Australia) Pty Ltd
P.O. Box 544, Potts Point, N.S.W. 2011

Pergamon Press GmbH
Hammerweg 6, D-6242 Kronberg,
Federal Republic of Germany

Copyright © 1984 Roy Long

*All rights reserved. No part of this publication
may be reproduced, stored in a retrieval system,
or transmitted, in any form or by any means,
electronic, electrostatic, magnetic tape, mechanical,
photocopying, recording or otherwise,
without permission in writing
from the publishers.*

First edition 1984

Printed in Great Britain by A Wheaton & Co. Ltd, Exeter
ISBN 0 08-029305-0 non net
ISBN 0 08-029306-9 net

Contents

Foreword	v
1. Meet the Lutherans	7
2. Martin Luther	19
3. The Lutherans in Britain	38
4. What Lutherans Believe	55
Important Dates	65
Further Reading	68
Useful Addresses	71

ACKNOWLEDGEMENTS

Thanks are due to the following for permission to reproduce photographs: Lutheran World Federation (pages 51, 52, 53), Mansell Collection (pages 20, 28), Trustees of the British Museum (page 31).

COVER PHOTOGRAPH: *A service at the Lutheran Church in Nottingham.*

Foreword

BY HIS GRACE
THE LORD ARCHBISHOP OF CANTERBURY

Christians in England know little about the Lutheran Church other than the beginning of Luther's protest and the story of the ninety-five theses at Wittenberg. Sometimes British Christians assume that Lutherans are much the same as Non-conformists in our own country. It comes as a surprise to them to discover the riches of Lutheran liturgical worship and its sacramental tradition. Church of England people discover a tradition very close indeed to their own.

As the celebrations of the 500th birthday of Martin Luther draw to a close, I am very happy to commend this book so that we may all become better informed about the Lutheran Churches.

+ Robert Cantuar:

1

Meet the Lutherans

The best way to find out about any Church and what it believes is to go to a church and take part in its worship. With most denominations in Britain this would not present any problems, but you might have to search before you found a Lutheran church to visit. However, we have an invitation for you: it says, quite simply, 'The Church Councils of the Lutheran Congregations in Nottingham have great pleasure in inviting you to attend a united service at the Lutheran Church in Homefield Road on Saturday, 31 October, at 6.00 p.m. in celebration of Reformation Day.' So let us accept the invitation and join the congregation as it gathers in the beautiful little church in a Nottingham suburb. The lights are blazing, the doors are wide open, and the members of the congregation are chatting to one another and shaking hands before the service starts.

Before they sit down, most people stand for a moment with their heads bowed in prayer. Since there is a little time before the service is due to start, we can have a look round and see what we can learn about the Lutherans. Perhaps we should start by looking at the hymn-book we were handed as we came in. At the front of the book are the orders of service. This tells us that the Lutheran Church is

7

liturgical, i.e. a Church which uses a set form of worship, like the Roman Catholic Church or the Church of England. In fact, if you have been to a service in either of these Churches, you will immediately notice a lot of similarities between the way they are furnished and the way a Lutheran church is set out. This is because all three Churches stand within a very ancient tradition of worship in Western Europe, and the layout of the church is part of the tradition. Lutherans, however, can be much more flexible in their worship than either of their sister Churches. The principle laid down by Martin Luther, and followed by Lutherans ever since, is that provided everything is done decently and in order the local church can arrange its worship in the way it wants to. In practice most congregations in a particular branch of the Church will probably follow a common order, though they may have some local variations. The use of a common order makes it easier for people to move from one congregation to another and by following an order of service that is based on an old tradition of worship, Lutherans show that they feel themselves to be direct descendants of the ancient Catholic Church.

This tradition of worship based on a set liturgy comes as a shock to some people who think that Luther got rid of everything 'Catholic'. What he and his colleagues did in the sixteenth century was to keep the old service, the Mass, but to remove things which had crept in over the centuries, such as prayers to the saints. 'Keep what is good' was one of the main principles, 'but get rid of what is against the gospel'. Above all else, the service and the preaching should be in the language of the people; so, whatever country you are in, it is the native language that is used. Even so, there are very strong similarities between the orders of service in different countries, so Lutherans almost always feel at home, even if they do not understand the language.

One other aspect of worship that unites Lutherans is their hymns. The Lutheran Church has been called 'the singing Church' and there is a great tradition of hymn singing in the services. Many Lutheran hymns are sung throughout the world and many are known in other denominations as well. Most Christians are familiar with such famous hymns as 'Now thank we all our God' and 'Praise to the Lord, the Almighty, the King of Creation', but they might not realise that these were written by Lutherans. Of course some hymns that are used by

Lutherans are not so well known elsewhere; for example, two very beautiful ones often sung are 'Children of the Heavenly Father' from Sweden, and 'So take my hand, dear Father'. Also each Lutheran Church has its own special hymns, like the Norwegian Christmas hymn 'I am so glad', or the great Lenten hymns, or 'Passiusalmar' by the Icelandic poet and pastor, Hallgrimur Pjetursson.

If we turn round in the church in Nottingham and look upwards we will see the choir gallery and the organ. Not all Lutheran churches have a choir, but almost all of them have an organ to accompany the singing; some of the greatest church music of all time has been written by Lutherans, such as George Frederick Handel and Dietrich Buxtehude. Without doubt, the most famous of all Lutheran composers was Johann Sebastian Bach, who wrote countless pieces of music for the Church and arranged many of the great Lutheran chorales. So great was his contribution that he has been regarded almost as a second Luther.

But now the organist has started to play and the congregation is becoming quiet as it gets ready for the service to begin. Perhaps we just have time to look quickly at the layout of the rest of the church. As we look over the heads of the people in front of us, the thing that draws our attention, because of its prominent position in the middle, is the altar, where the Lord's Supper is celebrated. In some old churches in central Europe the altar is in front of the pulpit, but this is quite rare; usually the pulpit is on one side of the church, as it is here in Nottingham. Somewhere in the church, perhaps at the entrance but more frequently on the opposite side of the altar to the pulpit, is the font, used for baptisms. In a way, these pieces of furniture sum up the main points of Lutheran belief: the pulpit for the reading and preaching of the Word of God, the altar and font for celebrating the sacraments, and the pews where the congregation sits. One of the most basic Lutheran teachings is that the Church is 'the assembly of all believers, among whom the gospel is preached in its purity and the holy sacraments are administered according to the gospel.'

The church has become quiet; on the altar the candles light up the cross and the open Bible from which the lessons will be read and the sermon preached. As the organist finishes the prelude, a door opens on the left and the pastors (this is the normal term for Lutheran ministers) who are going to conduct the service come in. There are four of them to lead this service; as we learn later, one of them is a Latvian pastor from Leicester, another is a German pastor from Bradford, a third is a Polish pastor from Leeds and the fourth is an English pastor from Corby, in Northamptonshire. The English pastor, who is going to lead the service, has been coming to Nottingham regularly during the past few months to look after the German-speaking congregation here because its former pastor has returned to Germany and the new one will not come for another two months. He has had to preach regularly in German and English, but as he welcomes us to the service tonight it is clear that it will be in English because that is the language that everyone present understands.

The introduction and welcome over, the pastor announces the first hymn, 'Holy God, we praise Thy Name', which was a Roman Catholic hymn originally, but which is beloved by Lutherans in many countries. While the congregation is singing the hymn we might observe how the pastors are dressed for the service. Along with the other things that Lutherans retained at the Reformation was the tradition of the pastor wearing special vestments when conducting the worship. In principle, he could wear his best suit if he wanted to, but the vestments help him and the congregation to remember that he is not acting just in a personal capacity but on behalf of the whole Church. Three of the pastors in our service are wearing a black gown with white bands hanging down from the collar; the fourth, the Polish pastor, is wearing the same sort of gown, but over it he has a beautiful white silk vestment edged with a deep border of lace, called an 'alba' – this is a special vestment worn only in Poland and it has a history behind it. For a long time after the Reformation, Lutheran pastors wore the same vestments as were worn by Roman Catholic priests, and this tradition has been retained right down to the present day in the Churches of Scandinavia and one or two other places. However, it died out in most places in Germany and Central Europe, and from the beginning of the nineteenth century the black gown and bands became normal, though in some places the pastors wear a stiff starched ruff like those worn by the aristocracy in the sixteenth century. Nowadays, especially in America, more and more pastors are going back to the traditional vestments of Reformation times.

A confirmation service conducted by a Polish pastor; he is wearing an alba

The opening hymn is over and the pastor has invited the congregation to stand. (Most Lutherans sit to sing hymns and stand to pray.) As he faces the altar, the pastor chants some verses from one of the Psalms: this is called the 'Introit' and it sets the theme for the service. Today, the words are from Psalm 46, starting 'God is our refuge and strength, a very present help in trouble'. At the end of the verses appointed for the day the congregation joins in by singing 'Glory be to the Father, and to the Son, and to the Holy Ghost, as it was in the beginning, is now and ever shall be, world without end, Amen.' Still facing the altar, the pastor leads the congregation in a short prayer called a 'Litany' in which he chants a petition, or request, and the congregation responds with the phrase 'Lord, have mercy'. There are six petitions, all to do with peace, but in some churches there is a shorter Litany, often including the Greek words 'Kyrie eleison, Christe eleison' chanted by the pastor. Luther kept these Greek words to remind Christians of the earliest Churches when the normal language was Greek. Then the whole congregation joins in one of the most ancient hymns of the Church, starting with the words sung by the angels at Bethlehem, 'Glory be to God on high, and on earth peace, goodwill towards men'.

The service now moves into another stage. The pastor turns and greets the congregation with the words 'The Lord be with you'. After their reply, 'And with thy spirit', he invites them to join in the 'Collect for the Day'. This is a short prayer on the main theme of the service, and it echoes the ideas that have already been heard in the Introit. As he turns back to face the people they would normally sit down, but today is a special occasion and they remain standing. Usually this is the point when the lessons are read from the Bible. There will certainly be a reading from one of the New Testament Epistles, and often this is preceded by a reading from the Old Testament. The high spot is always the reading from the Gospels; for the Old Testament lesson and the Epistle the people sit, for the Gospel they always stand. Today there will be a reading only from the Gospels. The passage to be read is John 8: 31–36 and this is also the text from which the sermon will be preached in a few minutes. However, you might be surprised to find that when one of the pastors steps forward he reads the Gospel in German; then a member of the congregation steps forward and reads it in what sounds like Polish (it is!); another pastor reads it in the Latvian language; another layman reads it in Estonian; finally, it is read in English. The reading of the Gospel in all these different languages is symbolic: the members of the congregation hear it in their own language, yet show that they are united by the same gospel. Immediately afterwards they demonstrate that unity when the pastor leading the service invites them all to join together in saying the Apostles' Creed. As we can hear from the people around us, most people are using English, but some are saying it in their own language.

Now we are coming to an important part of the service. The pastor announces the hymn before the sermon. It is called 'Lord, keep us steadfast in Thy Word' and was written by Martin Luther. It is often sung before or after the sermon in Lutheran churches, though it is not very well known in other denominations. The hymn has a very simple melody and some people sing it without the book. A few people are singing it in their own language – occasionally the words and music do not fit each other, but no one minds!

At the end of the hymn the congregation stands and the Polish pastor, in his white alba, greets the people from the pulpit with the words 'Dear friends in Christ, may grace and peace be yours from God our Father, and from our Lord and Saviour, Jesus Christ. Amen.' He then reads the text on which he is going to base his sermon and the congregation sits down. The pastor's alba has a special connection with preaching in the history of the Polish Lutheran Church. Two hundred years ago Lutherans in the south of Poland were harshly persecuted and their churches were closed. Congregations gathered in the hills or in the depths of the forests for services and the pastor wore the alba so that he could be seen more easily.

Lutheran pastors take a great deal of care in preparing their sermons. It is normal for them to preach on one of the lessons read during the service, and in some places the set text for the day is used. The pastor will have spent many hours studying the passage, often reading it through to himself in the original Hebrew or Greek. He will study commentaries to try to find out what scholars think that the passage means and he may read sermons preached by other people on the same text, but in the end it is always his own sermon; he is trying to make God's Word understandable to the particular congregation he is preaching to. (I refer to the pastor as 'he', but many Lutheran Churches now allow women to be pastors. I shall continue to use 'he' in this chapter because all the pastors in this service are men.)

Today the pastor is preaching about the Reformation and about what the movement started by Martin Luther means for individual people and for the whole Christian Church today. Lutheran sermons are always based firmly on the Bible and the preacher's task is to relate his chosen passage to people's lives today. It is because they take this task seriously that pastors prepare their sermons so thoroughly. This concern for understanding the real message of the Bible explains not only why there are so many great Lutheran preachers, but also why there are so many great Lutheran Biblical scholars. Lutherans emphasize the importance of theology – most pastors undergo five or six years of theological education – but the purpose of this study is always to enable the pastor to make God's message as clearly understood as possible.

When the sermon is over the congregation joins in singing another hymn. This time we have no difficulty in recognising it: it is a famous hymn by Charles Wesley, 'Love divine, all loves excelling'. (Although John and Charles Wesley were the first Methodists, they greatly admired Luther and many of their hymns are sung in Lutheran churches.) During the hymn a collection is taken; this year's offering is going to Hothorpe Hall, the Church's Conference Centre near Market Harborough. Last year the collection went to Christian Aid.

Today's service includes the Holy Communion, and the pastor now addresses the congregation with an 'Exhortation', a short address calling on them to confess their sins before coming to the altar. The people hear him say how necessary it is to confess their sins and receive God's forgiveness. Together they join in saying a prayer of confession and stand with heads bowed as he pronounces the words 'As a minister of the Church of Christ, and by his authority, I declare unto you the entire forgiveness of all your sins. In the Name of the Father, and of the Son, and of the Holy Ghost. Amen.' Immediately after this the congregation joins in singing one of the greatest Lutheran hymns, 'Now thank we all our God'. Be careful when singing this hymn in a Lutheran church: Lutherans sing the original tune which contains some different notes from the one normally used in English churches!

And so the 'Thanksgiving' or 'Eucharist' begins. On the altar is a flagon of wine, a cup and a plate with bread on it. Like Roman Catholics and Anglicans, most Lutherans use wafers of unleavened bread. The Eucharist begins with a beautiful responsive chant, going back over fifteen hundred years, called the 'Sursum Corda', beginning, 'Lift up your hearts'. It ends with the congregation singing an ancient hymn based on Isaiah 6, 'Holy, Holy, Holy, Lord God of Sabaoth'. In this church the altar stands away from the wall and two of the pastors are standing behind it, facing the people. The pastor who has been leading the service now says Christ's own words, 'This is my body' and 'This is my blood'. Lutherans believe that Christ is truly present in the bread and wine (the phrase they use to describe this is 'in, with, and under') but they are also interested in why he is present. Jesus has promised to be with his people in this supper, giving them forgiveness of their sins.

Everyone now joins in saying the Lord's Prayer, then, as the congregation sings another ancient hymn, the 'Agnus Dei', about a dozen people go and kneel before the altar. The first pastor moves along the line of kneeling people and places the bread into their mouths, with the words 'The Body of Christ, given for you'. The second pastor follows with the cup of wine, saying, as each person drinks, 'The Blood of Christ, shed for you'. The group remains kneeling until everyone has received the bread and wine and the pastor has told them to 'go in peace'. Several groups come forward like this; finally, when everyone has communed, the pastors give each other the bread and wine.

The service is now drawing to a close. The congregation sings Simeon's hymn from Luke 2, 'Lord, now lettest Thou Thy servant depart in peace', the pastor says a prayer and then gives a blessing. Now comes a very stirring moment. This is a Reformation Day Service and it is traditional for the congregation to stand and sing Luther's great and rousing hymn, 'A mighty fortress is our God'. It is a very moving experience to hear these people, from many different countries and singing in various languages, joining together in Luther's old hymn of praise.

The service is over, but the congregation does not drift away. As the organ plays a postlude by Bach, the people say their final prayers and go to the back of the church. Everyone shakes hands with the pastors and has a few words with their friends: a Lutheran congregation is rather like a big family. After the service tonight everyone is going next door to the church hall where there are tables spread with cups and saucers, plates and stacks of good food: continental sandwiches, cakes and plenty of tea and coffee. This united service takes place every year; during the rest of the year the services are held in different languages – German, English, Estonian, Polish and Latvian.

Being guests, of course, we do not know anyone, but one of the men from the congregation takes us around so that we can meet some of the people and learn a little bit about them. On the first table there is a group of people speaking to one another in Polish; one elderly lady has come 30 kilometres to be at the service. She tells us that she came originally from Warsaw, but that she was brought up speaking German as well as Polish, so she comes regularly to the services held in either language. The other people are Polish as well, and they come to Nottingham for Polish services and English services because their children have grown up in this country and speak English most of the time. One of the men at the table was brought up to speak Polish, but his home was actually in Czechoslovakia, where even to this day there is a large Polish-speaking Lutheran Church. The one thing that all these people have in common is that they came to Britain because they were forced to leave their own countries during and after the Second World War. If we had time to listen to the stories they could tell we would hear some tragic tales, but, although they might be rather shy to talk about it, the thing that helped them all through the difficult times was their faith.

Everyone in the hall has their own story to tell. There are German women who married English soldiers and who came to live in this country after the Second World War; there are some American students who live in a hostel just across the road and who study at the university; there is a Latvian man whose parents brought him to Britain after the war and who is now a lecturer; there is a lady from Nigeria. There are teachers, housewives, people who work in factories, old-age pensioners, middle-aged people, children. Whatever their background, whatever their nationality, this little church in Nottingham is their home, and in spite of all their differences, they belong together as part of the world-wide family of the Lutheran Church.

This service that we have joined in takes place every year; it reminds Lutherans who normally belong to different congregations that they are part of the whole family of the Lutheran Church. Although it was a typical Lutheran service, not all services are exactly the same; the biggest difference in Great Britain is that Lutheran congregations worship in various languages. Not all of these congregations have their own church buildings. The day after this service took place in Nottingham, the Polish pastor conducted a service for an English congregation in a church house in Leeds. Two old terraced houses had been knocked together to provide a pastor's flat, a chapel, a nursery and a social room for the congregation. In the afternoon the pastor had to drive over the Pennines to conduct a Lutheran service in Polish in a Methodist church in Preston. The congregation there is too small to have a church of its own, so it has an agreement to use the Methodist church at a convenient time. On the same day the German pastor was in his own hundred-year-old church in Bradford for a German service, the Latvian pastor held an English service in Leicester in the morning and a Latvian service in Birmingham in the afternoon. The English pastor took a German Lutheran service with an English sermon in a Church of England chapel in Derby! That same Sunday Lutheran pastors might have been conducting services in no less than sixteen different languages in towns and cities throughout the British Isles, in brand new churches on housing estates, or in church houses in the middle of old cities.

And what about the church itself, sitting there in a suburb of Nottingham? Well, if you came back three weeks later you would find the church hall packed with people at the annual Advent Bazaar; a week after that the same hall was full of English and Scandinavian people celebrating a typical 'Julefest' (Christmas festivities). This little church in Nottingham is typical of the Lutheran Church in Britain: a place of faith for people from many different nations.

From what you have read in this chapter you might gain the impression that the Lutheran Church in Britain is very much a 'foreign' Church. This is partly true: the majority of Lutherans in Britain have strong connections with countries abroad. However, the

Lutheran Church in Britain is not a 'new' Church since Lutherans have been living and worshipping in this country for hundreds of years. Perhaps you will understand a little more if we examine the history of the Lutherans.

Think about . . .

As you will have read in this chapter, the Lutheran Church is a 'liturgical Church'. What is your opinion about worshipping according to a set form of service like this? What advantages do you think it might have over the sort of worship used more commonly in the Free Churches? Are there any disadvantages?

Lutherans follow the Church year which starts with the First Sunday in Advent, four weeks before Christmas. One of the things that they use is the Advent wreath with its four candles. This is now used in many other Churches as well. Why do you think Lutherans use Advent wreaths in their churches and homes?

Find out all you can about Johann Sebastian Bach. Do you think that music plays an important part in Christian worship?

What is the point of the pastor wearing special vestments to conduct the service? Do you think that this is out of date and that it would be better for him to lead the worship in ordinary clothes?

2

Martin Luther

It is Wednesday, 4 May 1983. In the small East German town of Eisenach, not far from the border with West Germany, thousands of people have been arriving from all over the country and from abroad as well. Through the industrial suburbs they come, past the enormous factories that produce Wartburg cars, into the town centre, which has changed little since the turn of the century, with its cobbled streets, its tramcars and its picture-book houses.

The crowds are heading for the Wartburg, not a new model of the car that might just have been unveiled but the medieval fortress that stands high above the town. It was on this day, in 1521, that Martin Luther came to the Wartburg as an unwilling guest, 'in protective custody' we might say. But the crowds have not come to Eisenach to celebrate that event; they have come to take part in the services and other events that are being held to mark the opening of the celebrations of the five-hundreth anniversary of Luther's birth in 1483 – celebrations that will continue throughout the year and which will end around the actual date of his birth, 10 November.

East Germany is a communist country, nowadays known as the 'German Democratic Republic'. It is the part of Germany that was occupied by the Russians at the

Martin Luther: from a painting by Lucas Cranach, 1529

end of the Second World War. It has a population of approximately seventeen million, about half of whom are still members of the Protestant church. On this day, up there in the Wartburg, an unusual event is taking place in a country which officially teaches atheism: the celebrations in honour of this great Christian, Martin Luther, are being attended not only by leaders of the Church, but also by important officials of the Communist Party. In addition, the whole event is being shown live on Channel One of East German television. It is not just the Church that is celebrating, but the State as well. The government of East Germany has spent vast amounts of money on publicity and preparations for all the overseas visitors who will come to Luther's homeland to see the historic sites, for although Luther really belongs to the whole German people, most of the places that he knew well are in the East German provinces of Saxony and Thuringia.

While the East German government is celebrating Martin Luther as a 'great son of Germany', the Church's celebrations are for something much more than that. The Church in East Germany is remembering Luther as one of the greatest figures in the history of the Christian Church. Luther's importance can be seen in the number of books that have been written about him, probably second only to the number of books written about Christ himself. So much has been written about him that it is sometimes difficult to sort out fact from legend. In addition, Luther himself wrote a great deal. A hundred years ago an official German edition of his writings was begun: it has now reached almost two hundred volumes! In this chapter it is possible to give only a brief summary of his life and his importance in the development of the Christian faith.

To begin with, we need to know something about the country and the time he was born in. In Luther's day Germany as we know it did not exist. Instead, there were scores of different states, some large and prosperous, others small and poverty-stricken. They were all part of what was called the 'Holy Roman Empire', at whose head was the Emperor, chosen by seven princes called 'Electors'. Luther lived all his life in the lands of the Elector of Saxony, who, during Luther's early life, was Frederick, nicknamed 'the Wise' because of the way in which he ruled his people.

Not all the princes were as wise as the Elector Frederick, and many were harsh and cruel. In many areas the peasants were very restless and grumbled about the conditions under which they lived. They had to work desperately hard to make ends meet, and they often suffered famine and disease.

Everyone Luther met would have been Roman Catholic, and all around him he would have seen the influence of the Church. In the towns and villages were churches and cathedrals, along the highways were shrines to the saints, in the streets priests, monks and friars were to be seen. There were many festivals and holy days when lively processions took place and plays about Biblical characters or miraculous stories of the saints were enacted.

Like everyone else, Hans and Margarete Luther, Martin's parents, were church-going Catholics. Over the centuries the Catholic Church had produced many great scholars and churchmen, but in Luther's day most people were ignorant and superstitious. Although they went to church, the majority did not understand much because the services were in Latin. The main service was the Mass, at which, it was believed, the bread and wine on the altar were changed into the body and blood of Christ and offered to God as a sacrifice for people's sins. People went to church for confession: they had to confess their sins to the priest and were given a penance to carry out in return for this forgiveness. The greatest fear of most people was what would happen after death: they believed that God was a stern judge who would reward them with heaven or condemn them to hell depending on how they had behaved in this world. Even those who went to heaven had to pass through a preparatory stage called purgatory where the remains of sin were purified away. It is small wonder that many books and pictures and stained-glass windows showed the terrors of death and judgement.

When Margarete Luther gave birth to her son just before midnight on 10 November 1483, neither she nor her husband could have dreamt how famous the boy would become. Hans was just a copper-miner near the town of Eisleben, and although he worked hard and became quite prosperous no one in his family had ever been well known. The Luthers were fairly strict in the way they brought up their children. Some writers have suggested that Hans Luther was so strict that he made his son timid and unbalanced, but although Martin mentions being caned by his father there is not much evidence to suggest that Hans was exceptionally cruel in any way.

The Luthers certainly wanted a good education for their son. Hans was slowly becoming more prosperous and one way of improving himself was to make sure that one of his children took up a better occupation. The only way to do that in those days was through schooling. So, at five, Martin went to school in nearby Mansfeld.

Then, at fourteen, he was sent away from home to attend another school in the city of Magdeburg. This school was run by a religious order called the 'Brethren of the Common Life'; there they not only taught Latin and the other things considered to be important, they also taught about the Bible and how important it was to have faith in God. After two years there Martin moved to Eisenach, where he seems to have been very happy. He lived in the house of a very religious lady called Frau Ursula Cotta and there are many stories about his life at this time, particularly his love of music and singing. Some of the stories tell how he and his friends were so poor that they used to sing outside people's houses to earn a little money.

Eventually, in 1501, Martin's years at Eisenach came to an end. By now his father was quite well off and he had great plans for his son. Martin should go to university, study law and perhaps make a good marriage. Martin went along with his father's plans and became a student at the university in Erfurt. He was a brilliant scholar and received his Master's degree in 1505, but before he began his legal studies something happened which no one expected and which completely changed the course of his life. To everyone's surprise and to the great anger of his father, Martin gave up his studies and entered a monastery.

Today there is a monument marking the spot where Luther is supposed to have made the decision to join a religious order. It was 2 July 1505 and he had been visiting his parents. Perhaps it had been a difficult visit and he had argued with his father; perhaps he was upset because one of his close friends had recently died; we cannot be sure. But as Luther was crossing a stretch of open meadow near the village of Stottenheim he was overtaken by a violent summer storm. The stories tell us that he was almost killed by a flash of lightning which threw him to the ground and that in his fear he cried out for help to St Anne, the patroness of miners. In gratitude for his safe deliverance he vowed there and then to become a monk. On his return to Erfurt, against everyone's advice, he gave away all his possessions and went as a novice into the cloister of Augustinian friars in the city.

What made Luther give up a promising career with all the possibilities that his good education could bring? What lay behind his decision on the road to Stottenheim? It is very difficult to say, because

Luther himself does not say much about it. He had been brought up as a good Catholic, along with many other people of that time, but there was no suggestion of taking holy orders. One thing that is known is that Luther was one of those people who are sometimes very lively and enthusiastic, but who can also suffer deep bouts of depression; this lasted throughout his life and caused him terrible suffering. He had a very strong sense of evil and a fear of the Devil and when he was really depressed he found it impossible to believe that he would ever go to heaven. The Church taught that there was no better way of being certain of reaching heaven than by becoming a monk. Perhaps Luther had been thinking of this for years; he had gone faithfully to church and had done everything the Church told him in order to lead a good life, but nothing seemed able to give him the certainty of God's love that he needed. So, at the age of twenty-two, Martin Luther became a monk in one of the strictest monasteries in Saxony.

From the time he entered the monastery Luther's career seemed outwardly very successful. His superiors realised that he was a scholarly and intellectual young man and marked him out for promotion. He was given the opportunity to carry on his studies, primarily so that he could become a priest. A priest was in a very special position: he stood between ordinary human beings and God. Only priests had the power to turn the bread and wine into the body and blood of Christ in the Mass; only priests could offer these as a sacrifice; only priests could forgive sin. In 1507 Luther became a priest and the power that he now had frightened him. Here he was, able to do all these things because of the power that had been given to him, yet he was still as sinful as ever. When he celebrated Mass for the first time he was so nervous that he almost spilt the wine in the chalice. At the monastery he tried everything he could think of to find peace with God. The only way that he really knew was by trying to bring his body under control. It was his body that was sinful, so it must be disciplined; to achieve this he punished himself by going without food and even beating himself till he fell unconscious.

During the first two or three years in the monastery, Luther probably treated himself so badly that he ruined his health for the rest of his life. He might even have killed himself had it not been for a very wise and experienced superior, Johann Staupitz, who gave him careful guidance and advice. Staupitz realised that one solution would be to give Luther a lot to do so that he would not have time to worry about his salvation. He made sure that Luther was kept busy, especially with studying theology. By 1509 Luther was sufficiently advanced to be able to start teaching in Erfurt University.

Luther impressed his superiors by his hard work and in 1510 he was given the opportunity of a lifetime. He was to accompany a senior monk who was going to Rome on business connected with a disagreement in the Augustinian Order. Rome was the holy city, the place where the Pope lived and where St Peter and St Paul were buried; we can imagine how eager Luther would be to go there. But, after weeks of travelling, what a disappointment when he finally got there. It was true that Rome had beautiful buildings; the rebuilding of St Peter's Cathedral had just begun and there were many impressive sights all around. However, what impressed Luther was the corruption: here, at the very heart of the Church, he found luxury, greed and even worse superstition than among the peasants back in Germany. The Popes had a terrible reputation. The Pope was supposed to be Christ's representative on earth, but only a few years earlier the Pope had come from the notorious Borgia family whose name was a byword for scandalous living. Luther was thoroughly disillusioned with everything he saw in Rome and was only too glad to return to Germany.

Back in Germany, a change was waiting for Luther. Frederick the Wise had opened a new university in the little town of Wittenberg and needed professors. Luther was sent to this new and rather struggling university. In fact, Wittenberg was to become his home for the rest of his life and it is so closely connected with the rest of his story that today it is even known as 'Lutherstadt Wittenberg'.

Though Luther was busy he still had the same doubts and depression as before. He seemed to be torn apart; he was a priest and a professor, but he was also a sinner who deserved nothing but God's anger and the punishment of hell. His greatest problem centred on a phrase he kept finding in the Bible, 'the righteousness of God'. He knew that God was holy and righteous, but that only made things worse because he himself was not. How could a righteous God love a sinner like him?

Eventually Luther found the answer to his problems while preparing some lectures that he had to give on St Paul's Letter to the Romans. He began to understand what St Paul meant by the 'righteousness of God' and he suddenly realised what God's love was all about. He saw that there is no way in which a person can earn God's favour by good works, hoping to please Him and receive forgiveness: forgiveness is a gift that comes from God. That gift is seen most clearly in Jesus himself, especially in the crucifixion when he died in place of sinners. If only they would trust in God's love, shown in Christ, people could come to God like children come to their father, knowing that their sins would be forgiven. This way of understanding God's love is called 'justification by faith' and Luther said that understanding it was like seeing the gates of heaven open up before his eyes. From then onwards, everything that he read and studied in the Bible was turned upside-down; he looked at things from a new angle and it was not long before this became apparent in his teaching. Hitherto he had more or less followed the traditional way of teaching, but soon his students were struck by the way he stressed God's love and forgiveness. Not only his students noticed this, his congregation did as well.

It was not long before the whole of Germany became aware of this change. Luther had already been thoroughly disillusioned by his visit to Rome: everywhere he looked he could see how corrupt the Church was. Now, his new discovery of justification by faith made him realise that it was not just a matter of corruption: the whole teaching of the Church about how men and women could be saved from damnation was wrong. The emphasis was almost entirely on doing good works to earn a place in heaven and Luther now knew that this was wrong. How could he put things right?

What finally stung him into action were the activities of a Dominican friar called John Tetzel who was travelling around Germany selling indulgences. The idea behind indulgences was connected with the saints and their good works. The Church taught that some people, especially the great saints, were far better than they actually needed to be to enter heaven. It was as though they had exceeded the minimum requirements for salvation and had a surplus beyond what was required by God. Their extra 'merit' went into a sort of common fund called the 'Treasury of Merits', parts of which could be transferred to other people to help them win their salvation. Indulgences had originally taken the form of letters or certificates issued by the Pope or a bishop and sold to people so that they did not have to undergo a punishment after confessing their sins. Later, people came to believe that indulgences could be bought to lessen the time spent in purgatory after death. People still needed to repent of their sins and confess them to a priest, but by Luther's day this idea was being widely abused. Selling indulgences had become big business and both the Church and individuals made a lot of money out of them. Indulgences could be bought in advance to cover sins not yet committed, and they could also be bought to speed up the deliverance of friends and family from the pains of purgatory.

Another abuse of indulgences was connected with relics. People in the sixteenth century were obsessed with relics, which might be bits of the bodily remains of saints or things that had belonged to them. Many people collected relics; Frederick the Wise had a collection running to thousands which he regularly put on show so that people could come and reverence them. An indulgence could be earned by showing respect to these relics. The scandal was that most of them were probably false; there were supposed to be enough fragments of the cross of Jesus to build a small battleship!

Tetzel was rather like a modern commercial traveller. He went around Germany making outrageous claims for his indulgences, which had the authority of the Pope behind them. He claimed that the moment an indulgence was paid for the soul of the person for whom it was bought was freed from purgatory and leapt up to heaven. The Elector forbade Tetzel to enter his territories – perhaps he did not want any competition with his own collection of relics – but some of Luther's parishioners went to Tetzel to buy his indulgences. Luther was furious because by then he realised what a fraud indulgences were.

If you go to Wittenberg today, you will find that the Castle Church contains many monuments to Luther. One is on the main door. In the sixteenth century this door was the town notice-board. Public notices, especially those connected with the University, were posted there. On 31 October 1517 Luther posted a notice of his own there; it is

An engraving of the Castle Church in Wittenberg

commemorated today by a bronze replica of the original. The document has become known as the 'Ninety-five Theses' and it consisted of ninety-five propositions that Luther wanted to debate with other professors. To display a notice of this kind was a normal thing to do in those days, and lecturers and professors regularly held debates among themselves. For this reason, Luther's theses were in Latin, the language of scholars, and were not intended for the ordinary people to read. They contained three main ideas: a protest against the way the Popes abused their power, a challenge to them to free souls from purgatory simply out of Christian love, instead of for money, and a denial of the idea of the 'Treasury of Merits'. Perhaps the most famous is Thesis 67: 'The true treasure of the Church is the gospel of Jesus Christ.'

Luther may have intended these theses only for scholars, but they soon came to the notice of many other people. They were copied, translated into German and printed and circulated throughout the Holy Roman Empire and even beyond. Many people who read them agreed enthusiastically with what Luther had written. It was not long before the whole matter reached the ears of Pope Leo X. At first, he thought it was just a dispute between different orders of monks, but he soon began to take more interest when he realised that Tetzel was not selling so many indulgences and the money was no longer coming in (part of Tetzel's proceeds were going towards the rebuilding of St Peter's in Rome). Within a few months the Pope realised that he would have to deal with Luther. At first, he tried persuasion, then he tried to get Frederick the Wise to use his influence, finally he tried threats. He ordered that Luther be sent to Rome to answer charges of heresy, which meant that he was accusing Luther of going against the teachings of the Church. This was a very serious charge: heretics could be burned at the stake. Luther was now in real danger and he was saved only because Frederick the Wise protected him. Frederick demanded that the charges against Luther be heard in Germany, not Rome, and because the Pope needed Frederick's political support he agreed. Luther was therefore summoned to appear before an Imperial Diet (a congress) in Augsburg in October 1518. He was promised safe conduct to go there, but this meant little since safe conducts had been broken in the past on the grounds that promises made to heretics were not binding. Luther hoped that he would have the chance to explain his objections to indulgences, but the Pope's representative, Cardinal Cajetan, was interested only in demanding that Luther change his mind and accept the Church's teachings. Luther refused to give up his opinions and in the end his friends had to help him escape from the city.

As time went on, Luther became increasingly opposed to the Roman Catholic Church. Though it started with Tetzel and the indulgences, his studies convinced him that the Catholic Church had twisted the teachings of Christ beyond all recognition. In a public debate in 1518 with a professor from Leipzig, he even said that the idea of the Pope as the head of the Church was not found in the teaching of Jesus, but was an invention of men. People had been burned for saying far less than that.

The climax came in the summer of 1520 when Luther published three long tracts, or pamphlets, which set out some very revolutionary ideas. In the first, *An Address to the Christian Nobility of the German Nation*, Luther called on the princes to undertake reforms because the

Church was failing to do so. He argued that the Pope should concern himself with spiritual matters, leaving practical affairs in local hands. In *The Babylonian Captivity of the Church* Luther argued that instead of the seven sacraments taught by the Roman Catholic Church (Baptism, Confirmation, Mass, Penance, Unction, Ordination and Matrimony), there were really only two: Baptism and Mass. He said that a sacrament needed two things – a command by Jesus and a visible, outward sign; in the case of Baptism this was water, and in the case of Mass, bread and wine. But Luther went beyond this to deny the special powers of priests. He argued for 'the priesthood of all believers', saying that by Baptism everyone becomes a priest, though not everyone becomes a minister who preaches and administers the sacraments. Finally, in the *Freedom of the Christian*, Luther summed up what he thought the Christian life consisted of: every Christian lives his life in faith towards God and love towards his neighbour. Through faith, a Christian is the lord of all and subject to no one, but at the same time, through love, he is the servant of all and subject to everyone.

All this was far too revolutionary for the Roman Catholic Church and, with Luther's ideas spreading so rapidly, the Pope decided that something more drastic must be done. He issued a proclamation (a papal bull) threatening Luther with excommunication unless he admitted his errors. If he was excommunicated, Luther would no longer be able to preach or administer the sacraments. When this document reached Luther his reply was to burn it in public. So, at the age of thirty-eight, Martin Luther was excommunicated. So far as the Catholic Church was concerned, he was no longer a preacher or teacher who could speak on behalf of the Church.

Almost immediately after this, the Emperor, Charles V, summoned Luther to appear before an Imperial Diet to answer charges of heresy and subversion. The Diet was to meet in the town of Worms, now an important city in West Germany. If Luther accepted the Emperor's summons he would put himself in a very dangerous situation, even though he would be given safe conduct, since there was no certainty that Frederick the Wise could still protect him. However, Luther was determined to go and in April 1521 he appeared before the Emperor himself. It was a dramatic scene: here was Luther, a peasant, the son

Frederick the Wise, Elector of Saxony

of a miner, a monk and thought by many to be a heretic, and all around him were the princes and nobles of the Holy Roman Empire. By now Luther was a best-selling author – the invention of the printing press had made possible the mass production of books – and on a table was a pile of his books. He was asked whether or not he would take back all that he had written. In reply, he spoke some words that are now famous: 'Unless I am convinced, by Scripture or by plain reason ... I cannot and I will not recant.... It is neither safe nor right to go against one's conscience. God help me. Amen.' The result was a foregone conclusion: the Emperor proclaimed Luther a heretic and an outlaw. If he remained within the borders of the Empire after twenty-one days he could be killed. It was ordered that all his books should be burned.

Luther was in the greatest danger, and even the Elector, Frederick, had to be very careful with his help. The Emperor honoured his word and allowed Luther to leave Worms in safety, but shortly afterwards Luther 'disappeared' and everyone thought that he had been killed. What had happened was that Frederick had sent troops after Luther as he was returning to Wittenberg. They 'captured' Luther and spirited him away to the Wartburg Castle. While everyone wondered whether or not he was still alive, Luther was kept in the Wartburg under the disguise of a bearded German knight, Junker Georg.

Initially Luther was very depressed. The Wartburg was isolated, high on its hill above Eisenach, 'the land of the birds', he called it. But as time went on he found work. In fact, his 'exile' was put to good use. Friends who knew where he was supplied Luther with books and he began one of his greatest pieces of work: a translation of the New Testament into German. Until then the Bible had been available only in Latin, but Luther wanted everyone to be able to understand it, so he carefully translated it into the German spoken by the ordinary people of Saxony. The result was scholarly, yet in the simple language that people used every day. It was not only a Christian feat, but a national one as well. Before then German had been a mixture of different dialects; however, Luther's German was so widely read that it soon became the common written language used by scholars and business men.

However, there was a more disturbing side to Luther's absence from Wittenberg. Some of his colleagues wanted to go further than Luther in reforming the Church. Under the leadership of one of these, Andreas Karlstadt, the reforms in Wittenberg grew more and more disorderly. Churches were attacked and property destroyed. Eventually, at great risk to himself, Luther returned from the Wartburg in March 1522. He preached a series of sermons calling for peaceful reform and in the end Karlstadt left Wittenberg and Luther and his colleagues set about the task of rebuilding the Church.

Over the next three or four years Luther completed his translation of the New Testament, worked out orders of service that let the whole congregation take an active part and wrote hymns for them to sing. However, he was not allowed to continue his reforms in peace. The German peasants had been cruelly oppressed for years, and in 1524–5 they rose in rebellion and caused havoc throughout the states. They hoped that Luther would support them, but he was shocked by what was happening and instead of supporting them he called on the princes to suppress the rebels. Luther has often been criticised for this, but he wanted peaceful reform and was opposed to violence. Furthermore, he believed that it was the duty of the princes, as Christian people, to maintain law and order. The rebellion was put down with great thoroughness. Until recently it was the peasants' leader, Thomas Muentzer, who was considered to be the great hero in East Germany, and not Luther, who 'betrayed the peasants'.

When the Peasants' Revolt was at its height, Luther took a revolutionary step himself. He still regarded himself as a monk, and one of the vows that he had taken was that of celibacy. However, in June 1525 he married Katharina von Bora, a former nun who had left her convent. Luther was forty-two and Katharina much younger, but their marriage turned out to be a very happy one. They had six children of their own and at one time or another gave a home to eleven orphans. Their house was constantly open to all sorts of people and, although she frequently did not know where the money was coming from, Katharina managed everything with great thrift and skill.

As Luther travelled around Saxony he realised that the Church still had many shortcomings. Parish pastors were often ignorant, the people lacked knowledge of their faith, and wealthy people were growing wealthier at the expense of the Church. To discover the true state of things, Luther organised a 'visitation' throughout Saxony. He was shocked by what he discovered, so he decided to do something about it. To deal with the ignorance of the clergy and the people he composed, in 1529, his two famous catechisms or manuals of instruction in the Christian faith. *The Small Catechism* was intended for children, while *The Large Catechism* for adults went into more detail. Both books are centred on the Ten Commandments, the Apostles' Creed, the Lord's Prayer, Baptism, Confession and the Lord's Supper. They also emphasise that the responsibility for Christian education rests, in the first place, with the father as head of the Christian household. These books are still used by the majority of Lutherans today.

During the twelve years since Luther had nailed up the Ninety-five Theses the structure of the Christian Church had changed a great deal. The Roman Catholic Church was still dominant, but Luther now had many supporters, including powerful princes who would fight to protect him and the 'Lutheran' Church. A further development was that other reformers were also at work, especially in the areas that are now southern Germany and Switzerland. Some of these, such as Uldrich Zwingli, wanted to go much further than Luther had done, but he tried hard to reach an agreement with them about the meaning of Christian teaching. In 1529, at a discussion in Marburg, unity was almost achieved, but there remained a disagreement about the Lord's Supper.

In the 1520s the Emperor had been too involved in wars with other enemies to worry about Luther, but in 1530 Europe was threatened by the Turks, so the Emperor summoned an Imperial Diet in Augsburg, hoping to reunite the Church so that he could lead a military campaign to drive the Turks out of Central Europe. Luther himself could not attend the Diet because he was still an outlaw, but many Lutheran princes and notables attended, including his great friend Philip Melanchthon. During the Diet Melanchthon tried to reach an agreement with the Roman Catholics, but in the end it proved impossible. On 30 June the Lutheran princes read out a long document which Melanchthon had composed, clearly stating the doctrines that they believed. This document, known ever since as the *Augsburg Confession*, claimed that the Lutherans had remained faithful to true Christian teaching and that the Roman Catholics were in error. It stressed the doctrine of justification by faith alone and the importance of the Scriptures in Christian doctrine. In some ways, the reading of the *Augsburg Confession* marked the real separation between Lutherans and Roman Catholics. This change in the structure of the Christian Church is known as the Reformation.

For the remainder of his life, Luther continued teaching, preaching and writing in Wittenberg. During his lifetime he published almost four hundred works, including commentaries, sermons, tracts and doctrinal writings, as well as scores of letters to people who had written to him for guidance. He continually worked on revising his translation of the Bible and on writing hymns. Luther would have preferred the Church to be concerned with such things alone, and not to become involved in political struggles, but there was always a danger that the Emperor, who was a devout Roman Catholic, would try to stamp out the Reformation. To prevent this happening some of the Lutheran princes allied together in the 'Smalkaldic League'. Under their protection, the Reformation spread throughout Northern and Central Europe and even beyond to Scandinavia and Eastern Europe.

After a lifetime of dangers and difficulties, Luther died as the result of a stroke on 18 February 1546 in Eisleben, the town of his birth, where he had travelled to arbitrate in a dispute between two princes. He was sixty-three. His body was taken back to Wittenberg and buried there. Only a few months later Wittenberg was captured by the Emperor's troops. Interestingly, as a mark of respect, the Catholic commander refused to allow Luther's grave to be touched.

Although Luther was never the head of a Church, he had a position of great authority in the Protestant Church. If there were important questions of doctrine, then it was to him that people came for advice. When he died there was a great gap and for years there were all sorts of controversies among his followers, especially because some of them became more and more influenced by the teachings of John Calvin, another reformer who lived and worked in Geneva. Many Protestants believed that Calvin had taken Luther's teachings further and completed the Reformation that he had started. Eventually, owing to the work of two great Lutheran theologians, Jakob Andreae and Martin Chemnitz, the majority of Lutherans came to an agreement about what real Lutheran teaching was. They gathered together all the main documents which summed up the Lutheran faith into the *Book of Concord*, which was signed by thousands of Lutheran pastors and teachers throughout Germany.

Although there are still some Lutheran Churches which do not accept all of the *Book of Concord*, most of them acknowledge the *Augsburg Confession* and Luther's *Small Catechism*. The Lutheran Church is a 'confessional' Church, i.e. it maintains that belief, teaching and preaching are of greatest importance. It is this that makes it different from other Churches. While other Churches may have particular methods of government, special forms of worship, or certain ranks of clergy (such as bishops, priests and deacons), Lutherans do not. For Lutherans none of these things is central to Christian teaching. At the heart of what they preach is the doctrine of justification by faith alone, just as it was at the heart of Luther's own personal experience of God's love and mercy. So when Lutherans talk to other Christian Churches about unity it is this that they are concerned about first and foremost, and all other things are secondary. As the *Augsburg Confession* puts it:

> It is sufficient for the true unity of the Christian Church that the gospel be preached in conformity with a pure understanding of it and that the sacraments be administered in accordance with the Divine Word. It is not necessary for the true unity of the Christian Church that ceremonies, instituted by men, should be observed uniformly in all places.

Think about . . .

What does it mean to become a monk? Why do you think the Protestants did away with the idea of monasticism?

Try to find out more about the tradition of relics. You will find a number of references to them in Geoffrey Chaucer's *Canterbury Tales*.

Draw up a chart showing the most important events in Martin Luther's life. There are many biographies of Luther. Why do you think that most biographers concentrate on the earlier events in his life?

Martin Luther has had an enormous influence on the Christian Church. Find out about what he meant to men like Thomas Cranmer, John Bunyan and John and Charles Wesley.

Do you think that all the recent changes in the Roman Church show any of Martin Luther's influence?

3

The Lutherans in Britain

As we have already seen, 31 October is a special day for Lutherans. On that day services are held to commemorate the Reformation in the sixteenth century and, although he would certainly never have approved, these services often become a celebration of Martin Luther. On 31 October 1517 there were no Lutherans; then, Martin Luther was a Roman Catholic professor of theology in a new university in a small town in Saxony. On that day he could have had little idea of the effect his actions would have. He certainly had no intention of breaking away from the Roman Catholic Church and founding a new one. Yet today there are over 70 million Lutherans throughout the world and, after the Roman Catholic and Eastern Orthodox Churches, they form the third largest single denomination in the Christian Church.

The Lutheran Church is unique among the Churches in Great Britain. Although there are only 24 000 practising Lutherans in Britain, on most Sundays you could find a Lutheran service being held in any of sixteen different languages. They are held in Chinese, Danish, English, Estonian, Faeroese, Finnish, German, Hungarian, Icelandic, Latvian, Lithuanian, Norwegian, Polish, Slovak, Swahili and Swedish. There surely cannot be any

other Church here which offers quite the same range of languages or traditions. If you put them all together the Lutheran Church in Britain presents a very rich and varied picture.

In fact, it would be more accurate to say 'the Lutheran Churches in Britain' because each different language group is organised into a separate church body, conducting its own affairs and making its own arrangements for holding services, providing pastors and so on. However, over the years most of these groups have realised the importance of working together, and now they do so nationally, through the Lutheran Council of Great Britain, as well as regionally and locally. This chapter will explain how all these different Lutherans came to be here.

The chief problem in writing a history of the Lutheran Churches in Britain is knowing exactly where to begin. The logical place ought to be 1669, when the first Lutheran congregation was established, but that would leave out nearly one hundred and fifty years of history since the time of Luther himself. Although there were no Lutheran congregations in Britain during that time, there were periods of strong Lutheran influence.

Let us begin with money. Take a coin and look carefully at the words inscribed around the Queen's head. The words read: Elizabeth II D.G. Reg. F.D. These are Latin abbreviations which can be translated as 'Queen, by the Grace of God, Defender of the Faith'. Even many Lutherans are not aware of it, but that last phrase in the title provides a direct link with the earliest Lutheran history in Britain. The title was introduced in 1521: it was granted by the Pope to Henry VIII for his defence of the Catholic Church against Luther. Luther's book *The Babylonian Captivity of the Church*, which asserted that there were only two sacraments, angered Henry so much that he wrote a reply called *Assertio Septem Sacramentorum*, in which he defended the seven sacraments of the Catholic Church. Out of gratitude the Pope granted him the title 'Defender of the Faith', which English sovereigns have held ever since.

No doubt subsequent Popes wondered whether Henry VIII really deserved to keep the title. Only a few years later the King made an enemy of the Pope and set himself up as head of the Church of England. He tried to make an alliance with Lutheran princes on the continent and even tried to get Luther's support when he wanted to end his marriage to Katherine of Aragon, but he was not successful and England never became Lutheran in the way that many other countries in Northern Europe did. The reason is simple: in England the King's wishes were paramount, especially in matters of religion, and Henry did not really have any love for the Lutherans. He was very conservative in matters of religion and wanted to govern the Church of England himself. After the split with Rome, the Church was still Catholic in nature, but without the Pope.

However, there were many English people who sympathised with Luther but, because of the King's views, it was dangerous to admit it openly. Three of the best known of these were Robert Barnes, William Tyndale and Thomas Cranmer. Interestingly, they were all connected with Cambridge University and at one time belonged to a circle of scholars who met regularly at the White Horse public house to discuss Luther's writings.

Like Luther, Robert Barnes was an Augustinian friar; unlike Luther, he ended his life as a martyr, burned at the stake in Smithfield in 1540. William Tyndale was another of the scholars to be martyred; he is remembered chiefly for translating the Bible into English. (Although he was not the first to do so, his translation was the first to be brought into common use.) The third reformer, Thomas Cranmer, suffered the same fate, though many years after the other two. He became Archbishop of Canterbury under Henry VIII and Edward VI. His great gift to the Church of England was its liturgy, the Book of Common Prayer, and wherever you look in it you will find echoes of the Lutheran orders of service. Cranmer was eventually burned in Oxford at the time when Mary I was trying to make England Catholic again. None of these men was a Lutheran in the sense that we use that word today, but they were supporters of the teaching of Martin Luther and we can quite properly think of them as being among the spiritual ancestors of British Lutherans today.

As it was eventually settled under Elizabeth I, the Church of England did not become a Lutheran Church, but you do not have to look far to see Lutheran influence. It is there in the Book of Common Prayer, as well as in the Thirty-nine Articles of Religion, which are still the official basis for the teaching of the Church of England, though not held in quite the same regard as that in which Lutherans hold their confessions of faith.

Throughout the hundred or so years from the time Elizabeth came to the throne (1558), there was a small Lutheran community in London, but it had no church and no services. Many of the Lutherans were merchants connected with the Hanseatic League, the great trading federation of cities around the Baltic Sea. Their London centre was the Steelyard, near the Tower of London. During Henry VIII's reign this was one of the channels through which Luther's writings were brought secretly into England. Probably many of the Steelyard merchants went to local Anglican churches, especially since many became naturalised English subjects.

The history of the organised Lutheran Churches in Britain starts in the reign of Charles II. In many ways he was a contradictory sort of ruler; he was almost certainly a secret Roman Catholic and would have liked to have seen non-Anglicans allowed to worship freely, yet the early years of his reign were ones of great intolerance. In 1662 all non-Anglican ministers were ejected from their churches and in 1664 the Conventicle Act forbade any public worship that did not follow the Book of Common Prayer. Therefore, it may seem strange that in 1669 Charles allowed Lutherans to establish their own congregation, with their own minister and their own services. The reason for this has more to do with money and politics than it does with religion.

Charles II was an extravagant man and by 1669 he was very short of money, though not entirely through his own fault. Everyone has heard of the Great Fire of London and of how the city was rebuilt by such architects as Sir Christopher Wren. Rebuilding takes money, and to raise this Charles turned to the rich merchants of the Hanseatic League. They agreed to provide both money and craftsmen, and in the next few years many Germans and Scandinavians came to London. Almost all of them were Lutherans and naturally they wanted to hold services in their own language. A church was clearly needed but, bearing in mind the laws of the day, that would need the King's permission and that was where politics came in.

Not only did Charles II need money, he needed allies as well. Across the Channel France was becoming increasingly powerful. One possible set of allies lay in the Lutheran countries of Northern

Europe, especially Sweden. That may explain why Charles was very receptive when the Swedish Ambassador, Sir John Barkmann Leijonberg, and the Master of the Steelyard, Jacob Jacobsen, went to him to obtain permission to establish a Lutheran congregation. The outcome of their visit was historic: Charles granted them the site of Holy Trinity the Less, one of the Anglican churches destroyed in the Great Fire, and with it the permission to build a Lutheran church. The church was completed in 1673 and became the home for a very cosmopolitan congregation, with members drawn from several European countries and even one or two from America! It is important to remember the international character of this first Lutheran congregation, for while German seems to have been the common language of worship, the criterion for membership was not nationality but belief. Holy Trinity Lutheran Church was a church for all Lutherans in the London area. If this pattern could have continued then the history of Lutherans in Britain might have been very different, but, as it was, national feelings often overcame religious beliefs.

For twenty years Holy Trinity was the only Lutheran church in England, but under William III and Mary II the restrictive religious laws were relaxed, and during the next twenty years four more Lutheran congregations were established. In 1692 the Scandinavians withdrew from Holy Trinity to found their own congregation, and this itself split in 1710 when the Swedes left to establish their own church: in that year Sweden and Denmark were at war, and the Swedish members were not very happy when the Danish pastor prayed for a Danish victory! Meanwhile, two other German congregations had been founded, both in royal palaces. St Mary's was established in the Palace of the Savoy, and another congregation was established in the Royal Palace of St James by Queen Anne's husband, George of Denmark, who was himself a Lutheran. Thus the pattern for the Lutheran Church in England was established at the beginning of the eighteenth century: the congregations used foreign languages and were all located in the London area.

After 1714 several more German congregations were established. In that year George I became King of England and many German Lutherans settled in the country. This was accompanied by a great

Christ Church, Kensington: this typical German Lutheran church is the successor to the congregation of St James' Palace

increase in contact between England and Northern Germany. One of the new German congregations was St George's, founded in 1762 and still in existence. It has the distinction of being the first Lutheran church in Britain to use English, though the pastor who did so was reprimanded for this by his parishioners.

The pattern of large-scale immigration from Germany was repeated in the nineteenth century when many Germans came to this country during the later stages of the Industrial Revolution. This time, however, they came not only to London but to the north of England and for the first time Lutheran congregations were established outside the capital. Sometimes these congregations were not strictly Lutheran, for this was the time when several of the Lutheran and Reformed Churches in Germany were being brought together in united Churches. Not all the German immigrants approved of this, and in London six young bakers and their families who wanted to remain 'pure' Lutherans wrote to the Missouri Synod in America to ask for help. (This was a Church composed of immigrants from Germany who had gone to the U.S.A. to escape from persecution and enforced union with Calvinists.) This body sent a pastor who helped them to organise two congregations, known as Immanuel and Holy Trinity Churches.

Meanwhile, another sort of Lutheran work was beginning outside London. A young German pastor called D.F.M. Harms had become very concerned about the welfare of German seamen in British ports and he worked hard to establish an organisation which became known as the 'German Mission to Seamen in Britain'. He started his work on Tyneside and it was not long before other countries followed his example. A Norwegian church was opened in Leith in 1864, a Swedish church in Liverpool in 1869, a Danish church in London in 1873 and a Finnish church in Grimsby in 1880. Over the years that followed, many more such churches were established and there were also Latvian and Estonian seamen's pastors at work in Britain at different times.

At the outbreak of the First World War in 1914 there were nearly forty Lutheran churches in Britain. Of these, twenty-one were German, but the war shattered their life. There was a wave of anti-German feeling and many people of German background were interned and church property was confiscated. By 1918 only the Hamburg Church (as the original Holy Trinity Church had been known for several generations) was still open and there was only one pastor left. It took many years to reorganise the life of the German congregations and they never fully returned to the strength of pre-war days. Immanuel and Holy Trinity survived more easily than the other German congregations because they had become first bilingual and then purely English-speaking congregations. These two small churches were to play an increasingly important part in the story of Lutheranism after the Second World War.

The years after Hitler came to power in Germany saw another big influx of Lutherans into Britain. To begin with, many German Lutherans of 'Jewish' background fled to Britain. Among those who helped them was the well-known theologian Dietrich Bonhoeffer, at that time pastor of one of the German Lutheran congregations in London. He was later murdered by the Nazis in 1945. After the outbreak of the Second World War many more refugees came to Britain to escape from Hitler. King Haakon of Norway came here with most of his armed forces, which meant that several new Norwegian congregations were established, though these were only temporary since, with the Allied victory, most Norwegians were able to return home. During the same period there were Polish forces in Britain as well; though most were Roman Catholic, there were also a sizeable number of Lutheran. Unlike the Norwegians, many Poles stayed on in Britain after 1945, so the demobilised Lutheran chaplains set about organising congregations throughout the country.

When the war ended in 1945 Europe was full of refugees, many of them Lutherans from Eastern Europe. They could not return to their own countries because Europe was divided into two by the 'Iron Curtain'. Many thousands of these refugees found a home in Britain. Estonians, Latvians, Lithuanians, Hungarians, Slovaks, Germans from East Prussia, Poland, Czechoslovakia and Romania all joined the growing Lutheran community in Britain. They had lost everything and the Church was an important means of helping them to rebuild their shattered lives. Among the refugees were a few pastors, but in the early years they had to do the same sort of hard manual work as their parishioners, so they could do very little to build up congregations and church life. Later these Lutherans from Eastern Europe were joined by refugees from the Hungarian Revolution in 1956.

From the very beginning, Lutherans in Britain realised that they needed one another's support, but they also needed help from their friends abroad. At this time Germany lay in ruins, so the Church there could not give much help. But, fortunately, the Lutheran World Federation had just been established and came forward to help by providing pastors with salaries so they could give up their jobs and concentrate on church work. In the spring of 1948 the 'Lutheran Council of Great Britain' was formed, and by the end of the year it included representatives of the Estonian, Latvian, Polish and German Lutherans, together with the pastor of the two English congregations in Kentish Town and Tottenham. The Missouri Synod, with which these two congregations were linked, helped to provide money on a fifty-fifty basis with other Lutherans. Today the Lutheran Council is still the main agency for co-operation between Lutherans in Britain, though the Evangelical Lutheran Church of England (the Missouri-Synod-related Church) is no longer a member, and other Lutheran Churches have since joined.

The scene has changed greatly since 1948. Then, Lutherans had to hold their services in other denominations' churches since few congregations had their own buildings. Now, although this still happens in some places, most towns and cities have a Lutheran building of some sort, either a church or church house, which is normally used by most of the Lutheran congregations in the area. The Lutheran Council itself owns several places on behalf of the Church: the Lutheran Church House in London, the International Lutheran Student Centre near St Pancras, and Hothorpe Hall, a Conference and Retreat Centre in Northamptonshire. Since 1958 the Council has had an arrangement whereby the Lutheran World Federation appoints a tutor at Mansfield College, Oxford. The tutor helps to train Lutheran pastors, but also lectures on Lutheran topics in the university and so helps to make Lutheranism better known in Britain. The Evangelical Lutheran Church of England has its own training centre, Westfield House, in Cambridge.

Perhaps the greatest change that has taken place in the past few years has been the increasing use of English in Lutheran churches. With the passing of time, many of the refugees who settled in Britain began to use English as their first language; some married Britons and brought up their children to speak English. British soldiers who had been in Iceland or the Faroe Islands during the war or with the British Army of the Rhine afterwards married Lutheran girls. As more Lutherans from abroad came here to study it became clear that some form of English ministry was needed. Although some of these people joined other Churches, the majority preferred to stay where they felt most at home. The Evangelical Lutheran Church of England had been worshipping in English since the First World War, and from 1947 had expanded into a flourishing Church with congregations in many parts of Britain. In addition, some of the national-language pastors also realised that occasional English services were important. At some time or another, most pastors had to use English at services such as baptisms and weddings.

As early as 1948 the German Church of St Mary in London began to hold services in English, and eventually an English congregation was established. This is known as St John's and now worships right in the heart of London, with members drawn from all over the world, just like the first Lutheran church in the city. Several other English congregations soon developed in other cities and towns. Since 1961 they have been united in the 'Lutheran Church in Great Britain – United Synod'. Not all English work is carried out through this Synod; for instance, several of the German congregations hold regular English family services, as we have already seen from the first chapter. In Cardiff, English services were conducted for many years by the German pastor in a Norwegian church!

For more than three centuries Lutheran congregations in Britain have carried on a ministry that is unique among British Protestant Churches. In spite of many problems and setbacks they have survived. They are an important part of the church scene in Britain, not only because they look after certain groups of people and preach in languages that other Churches do not use, but also because they represent the world's largest Protestant Church and they can bring special ideas and insight into discussions between different Churches in such bodies as the British Council of Churches (to which Lutherans have belonged for many years) or in local Councils of Churches. They represent a world-wide tradition that many British Christians still know little about.

The future of the Lutheran Churches in Britain is in God's hands, as it has been since the days when the first English 'Lutherans' met together in Cambridge, only too well aware that they might end up dying for their faith, or when the Swedish Ambassador led a delegation to Charles II to ask permission to establish a Lutheran congregation. They will exist so long as God has a need for them, carrying out their own special ministry, but sharing with other Churches in Britain the task of preaching the gospel and administering the sacraments. Lutherans are not here as competitors with other Churches, but to help them in a common task and to share with them a great tradition.

Today, there can be very few countries in the world which do not have Lutheran Churches. From Europe, the Church spread to the New World through emigration, and to what we now call the Third World through the work of missionaries. The vast majority of Lutheran Churches in the world belong to an organisation called the 'Lutheran World Federation' which has its headquarters in Geneva, Switzerland. A sizeable minority of Lutherans (nearly fifteen million) are members of Churches that do not belong to the World Federation, and of these many are associated with a large Church in North America called the 'Lutheran Church – Missouri Synod'. In Britain, most Lutherans are connected with the Lutheran World Federation through the Lutheran Council of Great Britain, but one body, the Evangelical Lutheran Church of England, is connected to the Missouri Synod.

When the Lutheran World Federation was established in 1947, it was dominated by the traditional Lutheran countries, such as Germany and Scandinavia (which had been Lutheran since the time of the Reformation), and by countries where millions of Lutheran immigrants from Europe had settled, such as the United States. The first assembly of the Federation was held in Sweden and its first president was a Swedish bishop, Anders Nygren. Thirty years later, the sixth assembly was held in Dar-es-Salaam, in Tanzania, and the

THE LUTHERAN CHURCH IN THE WORLD

The emblem superimposed on the map of the world is the one adopted for the seventh assembly of the Lutheran World Federation in Budapest in 1984. It was designed by the wife of a Lutheran pastor in Hungary.

A world-wide family of 70 million

Europe	54 597 983
U.S.A. & Canada	8 930 581
Latin America	974 237
Africa	2 683 982
Asia	2 743 967
Australasia	577 577

These figures represent the distribution of Lutherans in 1976. Out of this total of over 70 million, nearly 55 million belong to Churches related to the Lutheran World Federation.

main speakers and leaders were no longer just Europeans and North Americans but included Lutherans from, among other places, Japan, South Africa, Indonesia, South America, and Tanzania. The president elected at that assembly was Joseph Kibira, a bishop from the Lutheran Church in Tanzania. The World Federation had truly become a federation of Lutheran Churches from all over the world, with their own traditions and ways of doing things, but sharing a common faith and not afraid to disagree with each other about the meaning of that faith in the approach to the twenty-first century. The theme for that sixth assembly was 'In Christ, a New Community'.

The Lutheran World Federation is not a Church but an association of Lutheran Churches working and co-operating together. The president of the Federation is not the head of the Lutheran Church and neither he nor the Federation can interfere in the affairs of member Churches. There is an assembly, usually every six years, at which the president and an executive committee are elected. The Federation's headquarters in Geneva are in the same building as the

A temporary school in Massawa, Ethiopa

offices of the World Council of Churches, which shows how closely Lutherans work with other denominations, as well as with each other. Lutherans have always been active in the many attempts that have been made to reunite the Christian Church, and most Lutheran Churches belong to the World Council of Churches.

The work of the Lutheran World Federation is organised in several departments which deal with different matters. For instance, Lutherans have always been interested in theology, and the Federation encourages co-operation between Lutherans of different countries, bringing together theologians and teachers from all over the world to study and discuss topics of mutual interest and importance. It provides students with opportunities for further study abroad and sponsors a 'Foundation for Inter-Confessional Research' in Strasbourg. The Federation also serves as a channel through which the larger and more prosperous Lutheran Churches can help their smaller and poorer brethren (and that works the other way round, too, for the bigger Churches can often learn a lot from the faith of the

Some examples of the work of the Lutheran World Federation

Building work at Ndzevane Settlement Centre, Swaziland

Constructing farm workers' housing on Majoda Farm, Zimbabwe

Provision of a clean water supply, Mishamo Refugee Settlement, Tanzania

smaller Churches), and through which help can be given for many other needy causes: money, clothing, food and medicines can be given for refugees, for relief of suffering, and for community development programmes throughout the world. Above all else, the Lutheran World Federation gives to Lutherans a sense of belonging to the rich and varied family that is the Lutheran Church in the world today.

Think about . . .

What difference do you think it might have made to the development of the Church in Britain if it had become Lutheran at the time of the Reformation? Find out about Robert Barnes, Miles Coverdale, William Tyndale and Thomas Cranmer.

Nowadays it seems unthinkable to us that one group of Christians would burn other Christians because of what they believe. What do you think were the reasons that led people to do such things? Can you find out about anyone in modern times who has died for their faith?

Do you think that the Lutherans in Britain were right to remain as a separate Church, or do you think that they should have joined one of the other British denominations, especially when they started to use English? Draw an equilateral triangle and write the names 'Roman Catholic', 'Church of England' and 'Reformed', one at each corner. Write the word 'Lutheran' in the middle of the triangle. What things link the Lutheran Church with each of the other three Churches?

Two famous Lutherans of the twentieth century were Albert Schweitzer and Dietrich Bonhoeffer. In their own ways they both gave their lives for others. What can you find out about them and their work?

4

What Lutherans Believe

From the first three chapters of this book you will have learned about the history of the Lutheran Church; while you have been reading you will also have learned something of what Lutherans believe. The purpose of this final chapter is to provide a brief summary of Lutheran belief and teaching. The problem, however, is the same as in the earlier chapters: so much has been written about Lutheran doctrine in the last four hundred and fifty years that it is difficult to decide what to put in and what to leave out.

Perhaps the best way to tackle the problem is to ask ourselves, 'What should an average Lutheran know about the Christian faith?' This makes the task very much easier, because Luther himself answered this question. We have already read of his concern that people should understand the main teachings of the Church for themselves, and it was for this reason that he wrote his two catechisms. These two books were intended to provide a simple basis of instruction in the essentials of the Christian faith in such a way that a man could teach them to his wife and children, and a pastor could use them to instruct his congregation. Neither book covers every single item of Christian doctrine, and for some things you will have to look outside this chapter. The bibliography at the end of this book will help you.

Nowadays, Luther's Catechisms are used mainly for instructing young people who are going to be confirmed. Confirmation in Lutheran Churches usually takes place during the years of adolescence, though the actual age varies from church to church and country to country. It is always preceded by several months of instruction. Although in some Lutheran Churches children receive Communion before confirmation, in most places it is normal for confirmation to be regarded as the time when people are accepted as adult members of the Church and admitted to Holy Communion.

In Britain the instruction of confirmation candidates is not always an easy task since a pastor's congregations may be scattered over a wide area. Usually the pastor will instruct the individual candidates as far as possible and then bring them together for a few days so that they can meet one another and discuss what they have learned. In the Latvian and Estonian Churches most confirmands are in their later

Confirmation candidates at a Norwegian church in London

teens, but this is not so much a rule as a tradition. Confirmation is always carried out by the pastor of the congregation, not by a bishop.

Circumstances and traditions may vary, but whether it is under the difficult conditions in Britain or in a country where Lutheranism is the most common religion (where a pastor may have dozens of confirmands at the same time), the teaching that the candidates receive will be the same. So let us open Luther's *Small Catechism* and see what it says.

To begin with, it is necessary to have a Bible as well since the Catechism is a summary of the main teachings of the Bible. The contents are: The Ten Commandments, The Apostles' Creed, The Lord's Prayer, The Sacrament of Baptism and The Sacrament of the Altar (Holy Communion). Most copies of the Catechism also have Luther's explanation about Confession and the 'Office of the Keys', i.e. the Church's authority to forgive sins. Many also contain his brief Orders for Morning and Evening Prayer. Each of the main sections has a short explanation by Luther that can be easily learned and remembered.

Everything in these five sections of the Catechism is based on the Bible, so perhaps our first question ought to be, 'What do Lutherans believe about the Bible?' To be honest, we could not begin with a more difficult question, because, as in most branches of the Christian Church, there are considerable differences of opinion about how literally the Bible should be taken. Over the past one hundred and fifty years there have been many advances in the study of the Bible, owing to our growing understanding of how the original documents were written, how contemporary people thought, archaeological discoveries, and the dramatic changes in scientific thinking. Lutheran scholars have been in the forefront of Biblical study, but they are very far from agreeing about the significance of all the material in the Bible. For example, how do we interpret the stories of the Creation or the Flood, found in the Book of Genesis? Some Lutherans would insist that they are true in every detail, while others would take a rather different view.

However, most Lutherans would agree on two important points about the Bible. First, it is not one book but a library of books in two sections. The Old Testament, which contains the sacred writings of the Jewish people, consists of thirty-nine books, almost all of them written in Hebrew over a period of a thousand years. The Old Testament tells us about the creation of the world and the human race, and about how God chose the Jewish people to be His witnesses in a world that had grown sinful and ignorant of Him. It shows us how the chosen people failed in their mission, in spite of the fact that God spoke to them over and over again through His messengers, the prophets. The New Testament, consisting of twenty-seven books, was written in Greek during a period of about a hundred years. It tells how God finally revealed Himself to the world in Jesus Christ, and how the 'New Israel', the Christian Church, was given the task of spreading His message to the ends of the earth. In the pages of both sections are to be found many different types of literature: history, biography, poetry, legend, myth, letters, laws, wise sayings, proverbs and books of doctrine. In all of them God is at work, speaking to His people and telling us important things about Himself and the world. The very clearest message that we have from God is Jesus Christ himself, and he is really at the heart of the Bible.

The second point is that the Bible is not just a book of dead literature, but has a message that is alive and full of meaning for today. For that reason it must be available for ordinary people to read in the language that they normally speak. A translation that may be hundreds of years out of date is not satisfactory; it must be in modern and up-to-date language that people can easily understand. To help people's understanding, scholars write commentaries which try to explain the meaning of difficult passages. Above all else, the Bible is not just a book to be read, but a message to be preached as well. The pastor must continually bring home to the people in the congregation what God's message in the Bible means for them.

Since the Bible is the story of God's dealings with the world, the next important question ought to be, 'What do Lutherans believe about God?' Here, there is no difference between Lutherans and most other Christians. In the first six centuries of the Christian Church, theologians struggled to work out a basic doctrine about God and during this time the three so-called 'Ecumenical Creeds' (the Apostles', the Nicene and the Athanasian) came into existence. Lutherans accept these as fundamental beliefs, so that they, alongside most of the other major denominations, are 'Trinitarian', i.e. they believe in God as Father, Son and Holy Spirit. The Creeds, which are based on the Bible, give us a handy summary of the Christian faith. In the Catechisms, Luther uses the Apostles' Creed as his basic statement of faith, so perhaps we too can do that as we consider the rest of Lutheran teaching.

The First Article of the Apostles' Creed speaks of God as being the 'Father Almighty, Maker of heaven and earth'. The way in which Luther explains this shows that it is much more than a statement that God made the world. He makes it clear that God is a living and personal God who takes a vital and continued interest in His creation. God is like a father to every individual, and He has not only given each person his physical, mental and spiritual life, but is also the one who provides everything that is necessary to sustain life and who keeps us safe from danger and harm. The word 'Father' sums up what the real relationship is between God and His creatures, and when he explains the first phrase of the Lord's Prayer, Luther tells us that God encourages us to believe that He is truly our Father and we are His children: 'So we are to pray to Him with complete confidence, just as children speak to their loving Father.'

This relationship between God as a Father and mankind as His children was established by God as basic. Unfortunately, it is broken because there is a spirit of evil in the world which shows itself all too clearly in the way human beings behave. Sin is not just the individual wicked deeds that people commit; it is the whole failure of people to live their lives in trust towards God and it can be seen in the way that people think and speak and act. Luther uses the Ten Commandments to show us the sort of perfection that individuals should aspire to: perfect love and trust towards God, shown in loving service towards other people. The trouble is, no matter how hard we try to obey these Commandments, we fail to do so, and the Commandments show us up as what we are: sinful in thought, word and deed. Whoever disobeys God's Law (and that includes all the commands in the Bible as well as the Ten Commandments) is a sinner, and since we all disobey God's Law, we are all sinners whose inborn tendency is to separate ourselves from Him.

The Second Article of the Apostles' Creed makes it clear that, despite human sin and our inability to trust and love Him as we should, God still wants to be our Father. In his explanation of this Article, which speaks of Jesus Christ and his birth, death and resurrection, Luther emphasises not the teaching of Jesus but the meaning and significance of his death and resurrection. Jesus was in every sense human, but he was also the eternal Son of God. His death on the cross was not just the tragic accident of a good man put to death at the hands of evil men, it was part of a definite plan by God to defeat evil and save mankind from sin. This doctrine, called the 'Atonement', is at the heart of the New Testament, but it is very difficult to understand. One of the best studies of the doctrine is in a book called *Christus Victor*, by Gustaf Aulen, a Swedish Lutheran bishop. Perhaps, however, it is a doctrine which is beyond our human understanding, no matter how hard we try. Luther does not try to explain it in the Catechism, but says that 'Jesus Christ saved us from sin, death and the power of the Devil, not with silver and gold, but by his precious blood and innocent suffering and death, and by his resurrection. Because of this, we may be part of his kingdom and serve him in everlasting righteousness, innocence and blessedness.'

The Third Article of the Creed speaks of the work of the Holy Spirit in the Church, and this tells us how everything that God has done can become our personal possession. Luther's explanation tells us that by our own powers we cannot come back to God from the separation caused by our sin, or by our knowledge of God, for sin prevents us from having a true picture of what God is like. Neither can we come to God by our own efforts, because we can never live up to what God demands in His Commandments. But just as God took the initiative in sending His Son to die and rise again, and in some mysterious way made it possible for us to be His children again, so He sends the Holy Spirit to make us aware of what these things mean for us as individuals.

The Holy Spirit works through the Church; there, in the preaching of the Word of God, he calls human beings to be children of God. It is here that we come back to the importance of preaching in the Lutheran Church. When the pastor preaches a sermon he is not just giving instruction on how to live a Christian life, he is calling on people to *be* Christian. For this reason, every Lutheran sermon has to include a proclamation of the Law and the Gospel. When the pastor preaches the Law of God, he is proclaiming God's holiness and pointing to man's sinfulness; he is calling on men to repent by sincerely acknowledging their sins and confessing them to God. When the pastor proclaims the Gospel, he is proclaiming the love of God, offering His forgiveness of our sins, and inviting us to live in faith in the community of forgiven sinners that we call the 'Holy Christian Church'. One of Luther's best descriptions of a Christian is that he is a saint and a sinner at one and the same time: a saint because he is God's child in faith, and a sinner because that is his natural tendency. We see this very clearly in the Apostles' Creed, which states that the Holy Christian Church is the community of saints in which there is the forgiveness of sins.

The Christian Church is something that can be seen and yet at the same time it can never be seen; it is both visible and invisible. If we talk about the 'visible Church', then we see it in congregations where Christians gather together to hear God's Word and celebrate the sacraments. On Sunday after Sunday God's Word is preached to remind Christians of what God has done to recall them to a life of faith in God's forgiveness. On Sunday after Sunday, too, the sacraments are administered. Lutherans celebrate two sacraments. Luther said that for something to be a sacrament two conditions needed to be fulfilled: it should have Christ's word of command and something that can be seen and touched. So, out of the seven sacraments celebrated by Roman Catholics, he maintained that only two were genuine – Baptism and the Lord's Supper. He wanted the Supper celebrated every Sunday, but there are still many places where this does not happen. Lutherans stress that when the Supper is celebrated, Christ is actually present, coming among his people to forgive their sins. Luther kept the tradition of baptising children and taught that through the water, used with Christ's word and by his command, the sinful man is put to death and the person is reborn into a new life in Christ. He inherits all that God has done through Jesus Christ. Baptism also has a meaning for daily life: Christians need to repent of their evil deeds and desires every day and begin afresh in the confidence of God's forgiveness. We could call this 'life in baptism' or 'life in the forgiveness of sins'. Luther himself said that when he was in the greatest despair he took comfort from the simple words 'I am baptised'. At a later age children are taught the meaning of their baptism and the main teachings of the Christian faith. They take on themselves the responsibility of Christian adulthood in the service of confirmation.

The Church is also invisible, made up of all those people, of many different ages, denominations, races and languages, who have faith in Jesus Christ as their Saviour and whom God accepts as his children. No one can know who is part of this Church because no one can decide which people have real faith in their hearts. What is certain is that there is no single denomination which can claim to be the true Church outside which there is no salvation for others. Only on the Day of Judgement will it finally be clear who belongs to the true Christian Church and who does not.

It is clear from his own experience that Luther realised how hard it was to live a Christian life, but he had also discovered how much help God gives to Christians to live from day to day as His children. The fellowship of the Church, the preaching of the Word, the administration of the sacraments are all means by which God protects and defends His people from evil. The Church is a family which lives under God as its Father, and He has provided the means by which His children can be helped and comforted in times of distress. When people are in great distress they can turn directly to God by praying, but they can also go to the pastor, who will give them advice and help. Although it is not yet very common, some Lutheran Churches have reintroduced private confession for those who want it, i.e. a man or woman who feels guilty about their sins can go and confess these to God in the presence of the pastor, who will declare God's forgiveness to them. This practice fell into disuse for many years, but Luther clearly wanted it retained because he included a section on it in the Catechisms.

A very important aspect of the Lutheran Church is the way in which it stresses the family and its life together. Although views are changing in this respect in the twentieth century, the ideal is still a strong family life. Marriage services are very similar to those in other Churches, especially the Church of England, with the couple pledging to love, honour and support each other. Naturally, it is hoped that the couple will stay together for life, but most branches of the Lutheran Church recognise that sometimes marriages go wrong and that divorce may be necessary. In these cases, everything is done to keep the couple together, but if that is not possible, then the Church tries to help husband, wife and children in distressing circumstances.

This chapter has given a summary of what Lutherans believe, but you probably still have many questions to ask. There is certainly much more to say about Lutherans and their faith and life than could ever be put in these few pages, but perhaps this book has whetted your appetite to learn a little more. I hope that it has made you more aware of one of the least known of the Churches in Great Britain and of what it has to offer to the whole Christian Church, both in Britain and throughout the world.

> Lord God, heavenly Father, we know that we are dear children of Thine and that Thou art our beloved Father, not because we deserve it, nor could ever merit it, but because our dear Lord, Thine only-begotten Son, Jesus Christ, wills to be our brother and of his own accord offers and makes this blessing known to us. Since we may consider ourselves his brothers and he regards us as such, Thou wilt permit us to become and remain children of Thine for ever. Amen.
>
> Martin Luther

Think about . . .

Several Churches practise confirmation. Find out how they go about preparing young people to become adult members of the Church, and what ceremonies may be involved.

Lutherans sometimes talk about the 'living voice of the gospel' and of Jesus Christ as 'God's Word'. How do you think these ideas are connected with the pastor's preaching in church on Sunday?

Sins and sin: are these the same thing? Do you think that the Ten Commandments are still important for Christians? Should Christians try to obey them?

Do you think that there is anything different about the way in which Lutherans think about the Church? Read some of the other books in this Christian Denominations series and find out the differences between the Lutheran Church and the Roman Catholic Church, the Brethren, the Church of England, and the Society of Friends. Do Lutherans have anything in common with these Churches?

Important Dates

1483	Birth of Martin Luther in Eisleben.
1505	Luther graduates as Master of Arts in Erfurt University. Becomes an Augustinian friar.
1511	Luther moves to Wittenberg University.
1512	Luther becomes a Doctor of Theology.
1517	Luther nails the Ninety-five Theses to the door of the Castle Church in Wittenberg.
1520	Publication of the Three 'Reformation' Treatises. Luther burns the Papal Bull. Scholars in Cambridge begin to read Luther's works.
1521	Luther at the Diet of Worms, followed by concealment in the Wartburg. In England Henry VIII becomes 'Defender of the Faith'.
1522	Luther returns to Wittenberg. Publication of the German New Testament.
1523	Publication of Order of Worship.
1524	Luther's first hymn-book.
1525	Peasants' Revolt.
1526	Publication of William Tyndale's New Testament in English.

1527	Luther writes his great hymn, 'A Mighty Fortress is our God'.
1528	Visitation of the Saxon Church.
1529	Publication of the two Catechisms. Marburg Colloquy.
1530	Presentation of the Augsburg Confession, written by Melanchthon.
1534	Publication of the complete German Bible.
1540	Burning of Robert Barnes at Smithfield.
1546	Luther dies at Eisleben.
1549	Edward VI's first Book of Common Prayer.
1555	Burning of Thomas Cranmer at Oxford.
1560	Death of Melanchthon.
1563	Thirty-nine Articles of Religion of the Church of England.
1580	Publication of the Book of Concord.
1618–48	Thirty Years War in Germany.
1660	Accession of King Charles II.
1662	Great Ejection of Nonconformist ministers.
1666	Great Fire of London.
1669	Establishment of first Lutheran Church in Great Britain: Holy Trinity ('Hamburg') Lutheran Church.
1692	Scandinavians establish their own congregation in London.
1694	Establishment of St Mary-le-Savoy Lutheran Congregation.
1700	Establishment of Lutheran Congregation in Palace of St James.
1710	Establishment of Swedish Lutheran Congregation in London.
1714	George I becomes King of Great Britain.
1718	Anglican Book of Common Prayer translated into German.
1738	John Wesley converted after hearing reading of Luther's 'Preface to the Epistle to the Romans'.

1840 onwards	Many more Lutheran Congregations established in Britain.
1855	D. F. M. Harms establishes German Mission to Seamen in Britain.
1914–18	First World War seriously disrupts Lutheran Church life.
1933	Dietrich Bonhoeffer serves German Lutheran Church in Sydenham.
1939–45	Second World War brings thousands of Lutheran refugees to Britain.
1947	Establishment of Lutheran World Federation.
1948	Establishment of Lutheran Council of Great Britain.
1954	Lutheran services started in Dublin, leading to eventual establishment of the Lutheran Church in Ireland.
1955	Lutherans purchase Hothorpe Hall in Northamptonshire.
1957	Ministerial Training Programme established at Mansfield College, Oxford.
1964	Lutheran Council accepted as member of British Council of Churches.
1978	Dedication of International Lutheran Student Centre in London by Bishop Kibira, President of Lutheran World Federation.
1983	World-wide celebrations of 500th anniversary of birth of Martin Luther.

Further Reading

Easier books about Luther

A Man Called Martin Luther by K. BENSON (Concordia Publishing House, St Louis).
Luther and the Reformation by HEATHER CUBITT (Then and There series, Longman, 1976).
Martin Luther by JUDITH O'NEILL (Cambridge Introduction to the History of Mankind series, Cambridge University Press, 1975).

Easier books about Lutheran teaching

Living in the Kingdom by ALVIN ROGNESS (Augsburg Publishing House, Minneapolis, 1976).
Roots of Our Faith by JAMES A. NESTINGEN (Augsburg Publishing House, 1979).
Studies in Lutheran Doctrine by PAUL F. KELLER (Concordia Publishing House, 1960).
We Believe and Teach by MARTIN J. HEINECKEN (Fortress Press, Philadelphia, 1980).

Books about the Reformation

Reformation Europe, 1517–1559 by G. R. ELTON (Fontana History of Europe series, Collins, 1963).

Religious Thought in the Reformation by BERNARD M. G. REARDON (Longman, 1981).

The Reformation by OWEN CHADWICK (The Pelican History of the Church: 3, Penguin Books, 1964).

Books about Luther and the Reformation

Here I Stand by ROLAND BAINTON (Abingdon Press, Nashville, 1955).

Luther by RICHARD FRIEDENTHAL (Weidenfeld and Nicolson, 1970).

Luther and the Reformation by V. H. H. GREEN (Batsford, 1964).

Martin Luther and the Birth of Protestantism by JAMES ATKINSON (Marshall, Morgan & Scott, revised edition 1982).

Books about Luther and his teaching

Luther's Works English language edition (American edition), 54 Volumes (Concordia Publishing House and Fortress Press).

Let God be God by PHILIP WATSON (Epworth Press, 1960)

Martin Luther by E. G. RUPP and BENJAMIN DREWERY (Documents of Modern History series, Edward Arnold, 1970).

The Righteousness of God by E. GORDON RUPP (Hodder & Stoughton, 1953).

Books about the Lutherans and Britain

Henry VIII and Luther by ERWIN DOERNBERG (Barrie & Rockliffe, 1961).

Henry VIII and the Lutherans by NEELAK TJERNAGEL (Concordia Publishing House, 1965).

Luther's English Connection by J. E. MCGOLDRICK (Northwestern Publishing House, Milwaukee, 1979).

The Lutherian Council of Great Britain 25th Anniversary Handbook (Lutheran Council, 1975).

The Story of the Lutheran Church in Britain by E. GEORGE PEARCE (Concordia Publishing House, 1969, obtainable from The Evangelical Lutheran Church of England).

Useful Addresses

Concordia Publishing House, The Garden House, Hothorpe Hall *(see address below)*.

The Evangelical Lutheran Church of England, 110 Warwick Way, London SW1V 1FD

Hothorpe Hall, Lutheran Conference and Retreat Centre, Theddingworth, Lutterworth, Leicestershire LE17 6QX.

International Lutheran Student Centre, Thanet Street, St Pancras, London WC1H 9QH.

Lutheran Council of Great Britain, 8 Collingham Gardens, London SW5 0HW.

Lutheran World Federation, 150 Route de Ferney, 1211 Geneva 20, Switzerland.